"This guy! I plead the fifth. This guy is nuts."
- Eminem

"Dope questions, man. Very insightful, very thoughtful."
- Guru (Gang Starr)

"You like a Psychiatrist or some shit? This shit is just coming out but go ahead."
- Mary J. Blige

"Definitely a real interview! Digging deep up in there, man. Not afraid to ask questions!"
- K-CI Hailey (Jodeci)

"The Wizard asked me for a copy of your magazine."
- Guy-Manuel de Homem-Christo (Daft Punk)

"You didn't wear your glasses, and you haven't carried your hearing aid. What else is wrong with you?"
- Bushwick Bill

"Peace and blessing, Brother Harris. Thank you for inspiring my words. Keep 'yo balance."
- Erykah Badu

"Can I see that pen?"
- Bobby Brown

"What else do you want to know? Talk to me."
- Aaliyah

A Taste of The Real Diddy
Sean Combs In His Own Words!

We're in the world of entertainment. Hype has always transcended the music, the entertainment, the movie, the actor, the actress, the rapper, the musician. It hurts you when you go and look for the hype. One of the things with me is the hype just comes, and most of the time it comes in a bad way. It's not the most appealing hype that you would want to get, but somehow by me making it through it, being strong, usually the hype turns around into a positive.

━━━━ • • ━━━━ • • ━━━━

A lot of things what you see is what you get. How I live, how I am. It's a lot of the personal things as far as me as a person, the shades off, or maybe being silly, acting silly, acting stupid. Some of that stuff doesn't come across as much. What you see isn't a facade of something fictional. What you see is what I am, whether you like it or not. It's close; it's a piece of what I am. It's not the whole component, but it's a piece of what I am.

Other Behind The Music Tales Series Books

N.W.A: The Aftermath

The Real Eminem: Broke City Trash Rapper

The Real Destiny's Child: The Writing's On The Wall

New York State of Mind 1.0

The Reasonings of Buju Banton, Bounty Killer & Sizzla

Magnolia: Home of tha Soldiers (Behind the Scenes with the Cash Money Millionaires)

The Real 213

The Real MC Eiht: Geah!

THE REAL DIDDY

HARRIS ROSEN

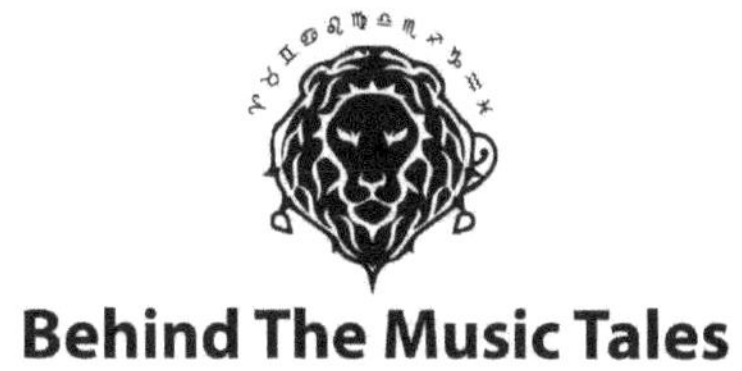

Behind The Music Tales

Published by Peace! Carving

Mr. Heller Press

Heller HQ

QB

Spadina-Fort York

Toronto, ON M5V 2B3

behindthemusictales.com

facebook.com/behindthemusictales

First Edition: September 2017

ISBN: 1988956005
ISBN-13: 978-1-988956-00-8
ISBN: 9780995307285 (ebook)

To my Son and Mother, for all their love.

CONTENTS

ACKNOWLEDGMENTS

Thank you, those who inspired me behind the scenes to produce this book. I appreciate your support, friendship, guidance, and understanding.

PREFACE

Puffy, Puff Daddy, P. Diddy, Diddy, Black Sinatra: whatever you choose to call him, Sean Combs has used his brain, finesse, and savvy to amass a net worth now approaching ONE BILLION DOLLARS!

The Real DIDDY *captures the entrepreneurial mind of Sean Combs TWICE in the summer of 1999. It is THE critical period in his life and fundamental to understanding the thought process that drove him to his current stature. The crossroads of life once completely in sync with the music business and the master shift to entertainment lifestyle capitalist.*

The GOOD

Puff Daddy is set to release **Forever***, the follow-up to his 7 000 000 selling take over* **No Way Out***. Sean Combs entertainment lifestyle empire and the influence that comes with lording over a corner of pop cultures are on a steady incline. Bad Boy Entertainment, Sean John, Justin's, and Notorious magazine is in excellent form.*

The BAD

A bevvy of ugly personal rumours aimed for Sean Combs essence. His sexuality questioned, and rumblings he is connected to the murder of Tupac Shakur.

The UGLY

Perilous and under the gun, Sean Combs is facing second-degree assault and criminal mischief charges, for erupting into Nas manager and Interscope Records executive Steve Stoute's office and allegedly smashing a champagne bottle over his head.

The Real DIDDY *presents over FIFTY MINUTES of Sean Combs IN HIS OWN WORDS culled from one exclusive interview and one invite only press conference. Meeting and greeting the main international media to transmit the rapture and persecution of being Puff Daddy.*

The questions and responses unveil a core understanding of who he is as a man, father, celebrity, artist, producer, entrepreneur and visionary. These critical personal reflections symbolise the turning point of Sean Combs life.

Behind The Music Tales *is a series which captures the mood and feel of the energy that surged from music in the 90s and 2000s. It presents exclusive, original interviews as an honest record, directly from authentic, creative forces, and is a clear historical document as close to the truth as one can get.*

The tale of Sean Combs real ascent is one we all know well. Born in Harlem, at the age of two his father, an associate of American Gangster Frank Lucas is shot and killed in his car. He was raised in Money earnin' Mount Vernon and graduated from Catholic school. He studied as a business major for one year at Howard University before resolving to pursue a career in the music industry decisively.

Diddy had witnessed friends, fellow Mount Vernon residents Heavy D and Eddie F, develop the Untouchables Entertainment Group, and Heavy D got him in the door of Uptown Records, where he began to climb the ladder of success on ground level as a mail room intern. Through hard work and dedication, he made himself known and was instrumental in forging the groundbreaking bad boy image of Jodeci. Behind the scenes of New York City's renowned nightlife scene as a party promoter, he crafted unique, special events formulated by positive energy, karma, and vibes, and the people followed. Sadly heartbreak ensued. He partnered with Heavy D to raise money, and awareness for AIDS charities and nine people died in a stampede rushing to enter a celebrity basketball game.

Two steps forward and one step back, facing civil suits and losing sleep. Diddy put his head down and committed to making Mary J. Blige and the rest of the Uptown Records roster stars. Mary J. Blige assumed her role and became the Queen of Hip-Hop Soul, Diddy became more aggressive in his pursuit of creative control over the roster clashing with label head honcho Andre Harrell too many times and got fired.

Bad Boy Entertainment was born in 1993 with Sean Combs as President. It was the dawn of a new era, one that Diddy himself had helped to paint with a cock-sure confidence. He quickly began to scale levels on the ladder of success with classic singles by The Notorious B.I.G., Craig Mack, 112, Total, Faith Evans, Mase and The Lox. Over the next two years, Bad Boy sold millions of albums while reconstructing the pop culture and urban music landscape. Sadly, The Notorious B.I.G. was killed in the spring of 1997.

Two steps forward and one step back, again. He doubled down on himself and reconstructed his upcoming solo album, **Hell Up In Harlem***, to* **No Way Out***, a thoughtful harmonious hook laden clash in standard samples and interpolations of days gone by, paying tribute to The Notorious B.I.G., spiked with controversial lyrics and honest emotions. It entered the U.S. and Canada charts at number one selling over 7 000 000 million copies in the U.S. Bad Boy and its cultural influence holding strong sway over the entire music industry catapulting Diddy to 40th on the Forbes highest paid entertainers list, resulting in a powerful push back by the Art Form of Hip-Hop itself.*

A deep-rooted love and devotion to music had Diddy two steps forward and one step back, again, however, by this time he had begun to diversify. After his movements within the music business industry, Diddy had spread his wings into complimentary offshoots of his fans lifestyle by opening his restaurant, Justin's, establishing clothing brand Sean John, and buying the Notorious magazine. Movies, charities and the class of opportunities celebrities often field to lie in the wings. His meticulously devised reputation as significant as the music, he attacked Steve Stoute in his office in retaliation for what he termed a blasphemous portrayal in Nas's "Hate Me Now" video, and accounts of a broken champagne bottle, jaw and arm emerged.

*In the summer of 1999, Puffy Daddy was preparing for the launch of his second solo album, **Forever**. In a world where hype had transcended the music, **Forever** was a far-reaching approach by Sean Combs with his shades off, opening up to give people a taste of his personal life. Its canvas is brimming with love, happiness, hurt, sex, drugs, rock n' roll, rap, and the various roles they played in his life.*

The evolution of Diddy had spawned a staggering number of vicious rumours directed at his core. Notably questioning his sexuality, and identifying him as the individual who funded the murder of the Tupac Shakur that beget the death of The Notorious B.I.G. On top of this, the music industry was served notice on the heels of Shawn Fanning's recent beta introduction of Napster and the subsequent emergence of widespread file sharing.

*The first interview featured in **The Real DIDDY** was in New York City, June 23, 1999. Major international media was invited and flew to the Big Apple for a special event press conference, select one-on-one interviews, upscale dinner and private open bar party with DJ Kid Capri, hosted by Puff Daddy.*

The second source is an invite only press conference in Toronto, Canada, July 30, 1999. Puff Daddy was in the city *to promote the upcoming release of **Forever** and participate on the weekend Caribana parade and festivities. His next artist, discovered by B.I.G.'s DJ Clark Kent, Shyne, amongst an entourage five Escalades by his side.*

Five months later inside Club New York, on December 27, 1999, Diddy, his then girlfriend Jennifer Lopez, and Shyne were involved in an altercation that escalated over a spilt drink. Diddy was seen firing a gunshot into the ceiling, and Shyne fired a semi-automatic handgun wounding three bystanders. They fled in an SUV running 11 lights and Diddy allegedly bribed his driver to take the fall.

Sean Combs was charged with four counts of illegal possession of a gun and bribing his driver. Shyne received eight counts, including attempted murder, assault, and reckless endangerment. Diddy retained Johnnie Cochrane and acquitted of all charges in March 2001. Shyne was convicted of five counts, sentenced to ten years. Shortly after, Puff Daddy put the drama behind him and changed his name to P. Diddy.

*The 12th book of the **Behind The Music Tales** series, **The Real DIDDY** unmasks the man behind the sunglasses and unravels the all or nothing at all spirit of Sean Combs, in his own words.*

Enjoy!

Harris Rosen

THE REAL DIDDY

CHAPTER 1

LARGER THAN LIFE

Everything you do has to be big.

Diddy: I mean, everything I do has to be big. That's the word, the way you said it. If I don't go all the way with it, I don't go at all. I don't half-ass. I do it 100%. I go all out.

Why does hype sometimes transcend the music?

Diddy: We're in the world of entertainment. Hype has always transcended the music, the entertainment, the movie, the actor, the actress, the rapper, the musician. It hurts you when you go and look for the hype. One of the things with me is the hype just comes, and most of the time it comes in a bad way. It's not the most appealing hype that you would want to get, but somehow by me making it through it, being strong, usually the hype turns around into a positive.

Your videos are larger than life. Are you ever going to decide to do a movie, and is that a reflection of yourself?

Diddy: Yeah, I've always liked things big. I've always been a big person type of person. That's the way I have always thought. I was always a dreamer, and I dream in big vision. I always try to do things that people

1

wouldn't expect us to do and things that they say you can't do. At this hour, I'm gonna pick up one of these films offers that I've gotten. As you know, I was supposed to do a film with Oliver Stone. (Diddy was slated to play backup Quarterback Willie Beaman in **Any Given Sunday**. Jamie Foxx filled the role.) They kept pushing it back.

I decided I want to be an artist still and not put out an album in 2001 because I had a movie out. Right after I finish this album, I'm gonna go on tour. If I don't go on tour right away, I may squeeze a movie in, but I have a movie in production at Miramax called **King Suckerman**, which I'm producing. It's adapted from a book that George Pelecanos wrote, and it's through Miramax, and it's the first Bad Boy Films project, and I may take a small role in there also.

I hear rumours you're developing a Saturday morning cartoon with the Fox network.

Diddy: Yeah. One of my favourite cartoons was Fat Albert and the Cosby Kids. We have a Puff Daddy and the Family cartoon. I can get it on the air if I stay out of trouble. The networks that sponsor us feel like I'm safe out there, all right.

What can we expect from the cartoon?

Diddy: You can expect life; kids making a lot of mistakes and overcoming them. A younger version of me. It's about my childhood, but it's about every kid's childhood. It's something that every kid can relate to.

Why is it the things that you are doing now are so lucky, whereas the artists in the past like MC Hammer, who has tried different venues, failed?

Diddy: I can't speak for other people. I can speak for me. I just get into something to win. I just refuse to lose. I'm the type of person I'm not going to give up. I'm not gonna lose. That thought doesn't come in my mind. I'm not saying that I can't lose, not being cocky or arrogant, it's that's the way my thought process is. It's only one way.

CHAPTER 2

MOGUL

Talk about the cross-pollination of what you're doing with music, fashion and media.

Diddy: Everything that I do is all intertwined. It's all a part of the culture. It's all a part of the lifestyle. From the clothes to the food, to the music, to the movies. I love entertaining people, and all of that's a part of the entertainment, even the way people dress is a part of entertainment in some way, shape or form. Even with the magazine, it's a part of entertainment. I'm a true entertainer, but, at the same time, a businessman and all of these things fall under that umbrella of what my goals are as far as making people happy.

Have you always had an entrepreneurial mind?

Diddy: I've had a dream of mine, always dreaming and always had one of mine, like, literally I used to cry every time I would lose. I was never a good loser. Same thing as an adult, I don't like the way that feels, so I do everything to make sure that I don't cry.

Is the clothing line entertainment?

Diddy: It's a part of the entertainment. When you entertain yourself you get dressed before you go to entertain, you put on a nice outfit, and before you stop to have dinner, so you can eat at my restaurant. I got my own Puffy world going on. You want to read some magazines -

Most of us here work for magazines or newspapers, but you're a magazine publisher. How is Notorious coming? It had one issue before you took over the reigns.

Diddy: Yeah, they had two issues before, they had three issues. One of the issues I was on before I purchased the majority of the magazine. I just like the way it was put together. Usually, when you see a new magazine it's not put together, presentation of it doesn't look up to par. This had an artistic presentation. I liked the way everything was laid out. I liked the vibe of the editor, and more importantly, the name of it was Notorious.

Your first issue, you made mention of the fact you were dedicating Notorious to Notorious B.I.G.

Diddy: That's the reason I bought it because it Big's name on it, to be honest.

What do you hope to do with it? Do you have plans?

Diddy: Yeah. I feel like the media is in charge of putting out much information. So many vibes. I want to be a positive magazine. I want to put out positive things on people not just controversial stuff. I want to put out things about people that are breaking the rules, people that are living on the edge, people of my generation, entertainment and lifestyle, that are doing things differently. When I say breaking the rules, doing things different, not the same regular way. We have Chris Rock on the cover this month. We have Jennifer Lopez on the cover next month, and we gonna take it step-by-step.

How involved are you?

Diddy: I'm very involved. I'm usually the final say. I let the editor, and everybody put everything together, and I glance over and read it and give my opinions. Sometimes they listen, sometimes they don't. I didn't like the first issue. I liked the second issue better, and I'm gonna love the third issue even more. It's a learning process for me; getting the distribution and circulation up. I'm going on a thirty city tour, and I'm also gonna be stopping at some places, in some retail places.

Have you discussed story ideas?

Diddy: Yeah. They give me a bunch of ideas and at least let me pick who is on the cover.

What's the name of the restaurant?

Diddy: Justin's.

Is it a chain?

Diddy: Yes, not a chain but I have one in New York,

one in Atlanta, and I'm gonna be opening one in Chicago. It's named Justin's after my son.

If I walk in what would it be?

Diddy: It's a fine dining atmosphere. It reflects the way I run all my businesses; it runs a tight ship. It represents Black food. You have Italian food, Caribbean food; you have Chinese food, Greek food; this is Black food. It's food for the soul.

Do you see yourself building a building and naming it after yourself?

Diddy: I don't know if I would build a building and name it after myself. I do what I do. I don't know about that. All the stuff I do I'm not spread out all over the place. Everything I do has to do with entertainment, and I love entertaining. I'll probably stick to entertainment, to doing business ventures in entertainment, that's what I love to do.

CHAPTER 3

THE ART OF CROSSOVER

What are your thoughts on being able to crossover playing straight without compromising what you do?

Diddy: I think that I'm blessed with having to do that. I've been tempted to go ahead and make this type of record, make that type of record, and I've got that fanbase. I'll probably say that I'm one of the first cats that are played before a Jay-Z record and after a Mos Def record in the club, whether it's the Benjamins, or stuff I did with Biggie, or stuff I did with KRS-One. People always try to push me there. 'He's commercial.' But then the reality of it is we can't argue that too much because he did rap with KRS-One and KRS-One ain't wack, right? Nas wanted to do a record with him. He has produced for Jay-Z and Biggie, and he is responsible for at least 40% of the records we dance to in the clubs, in an underground or an above ground club. I just try to make music to entertain people. I'm not trying to be the coolest cat in the streets, and I'm not trying to be the most pop rap artist. I'm just trying to make you move, or make you mad, or make you cry, or bring some emotion out of you.

It must feel great that you're already on the cover of

GQ with Jerry Seinfeld.

Diddy: It's beautiful. I'm on the cover of GQ, which was a big honour for me because of everybody, every kid that was into fashion always dreamed, especially a male. I wish that were me up there one day doing the GQ pose and everything, but I made sure at the same time I accepted to do GQ that I did The Source also. I made sure that I did The Source, and then I made sure that after The Source I do Blaze. In order for me to do Rolling Stone, I'll do Blaze. I try to even it out, so the fans don't get confused. I'm trying to take it to the next level, so maybe some readers that read GQ that don't listen to rap or don't understand it, they're reading about a person. It just so happens they may pick up a CD of mine, and they'll listen to my music, then they'll hear somebody better than me, and they'll hear Nas, and they'll hear Jay-Z or Biggie. I'm the introductory level. Overall, I view myself as an all-around entertainer.

CHAPTER 4

BAD BOY

Talk about your organisation and the people you surround yourself.

Diddy: I try to surround myself with people that have great follow through, that have passion, that wants to be something in life, want to be something in the future. That has a certain drive about themselves, so most of the people that I've hired are young people that don't have College degrees, basically have a High-School degree, don't have any previous experience. They wanted it so bad. They wanted it because they love the music, and they want it so bad.

You're back with Andre Harrell.

Diddy: Me and Andre never left each other. We were always friends. Back in the days with Uptown, he fired me. After running a record company, I can understand why he fired me. Me not understanding the politics and the whole big picture and getting on his nerves. Right now, I have ten Puffy's in my company, so I'm getting that back ten times fold. He taught me almost everything I knew, to be honest. In order to have somebody see eye to eye with me, to help me run my company, he was the best choice, and luckily things with him and Motown didn't work out, so I was able to get him.

What do Benny Medina and Andre Harrell add to the whole mix? You surround yourself with them.

Diddy: I surround myself with a major team of people because I feel like you can spread yourself too thin. It's gotten to a point with all the companies, whether it's the magazine or restaurant, the charity organisation, Bad Boy Technology, the clothing line, the record company. All of that is overwhelming if I had to run all of that. My philosophy has been to train people with my philosophy, my vibe, and my passion, and then give them free reign and let them do their thing. Let them lose money, let them make money, and be there as support. Benny, he manages me as an artist, is also instrumental in taking my artistry and going out and doing other things like puffdaddy.com, which is a major website that's gonna be launching the 2nd, in a couple of days we gonna launch that website. He manages me as an artist. Then you have Andre. He runs the record company now. He taught me everything that I know. He got a really bad rap at Motown. At a place that had no hot acts, and they expected him to have hot acts, and I know how hot he is. And he's helped Bad Boy come to the point that as we were getting so many acts and I was getting big, it could have got to a situation to whereas I would have had to give up one or the other, and he made it possible for me to do both.

Are there any young artists you're developing now?

Diddy: Yes, Carl Thomas is my 2000 version, my 2000 answer of Marvin Gaye.

How old is he?

Diddy: He's 26.

Isn't there a kid you have coming out?

Diddy: Jerome.

When is he dropping?

Diddy: He should drop around the top of 2000. He's 11. His lawyer brought me a tape, a video tape.

Are you always out scouting everywhere?

Diddy: Yeah, I have A&R people. We're always out there trying to find the new latest hottest thing. We're all in competition. All the labels are competing trying to find the new hottest flavour.

CHAPTER 5

FOREVER

What's **Forever** on?

Diddy: The album is about a lot of different journeys that I go through. The album is not that difficult; it's simple. There's love, happiness, pain, hurt, sex, drugs, rock n' roll, rap, all of that. All of that stuff intertwined in one, it's a big 'ol movie.

What can expect with **Forever**?

Diddy: **Forever** is the sequel, I have to say, the sequel to **No Way Out**. People that like **No Way Out** or loved **No Way Out**, they definitely will love **Forever**. People that didn't like **No Way Out**, they'll love **Forever**. It's me stepping up my game. I've gotten better lyrically and gotten better performance wise; production has stepped up. It's still a story, it's still just my life, but through the eyes of everybody that can relate to things that I go through. The same things we all go through some of the similar things. It's just really that story of survival. Somebody that's not gonna stop.

Is it still danceable?

Diddy: Oh yeah, definitely still is danceable.

One of the ingenious things about your production is

your ability to take an old 80's hook and toss it into a mix. Something that you're familiar with but it sounds new when you do it.

Are you doing that on **Forever**?

Diddy: That was a year thing. For like a year, there were a lot of hooks that were jacked. Everybody was jacking hooks in this year. You were hearing the hooks in records all over the place. I didn't mess around with any hooks. I always have sampled records but I never... On this one, I haven't messed with any hooks.

On **Forever**, you have a Drum and Bass song. What drew you into the Drum and Bass sound and why did you come up with the song?

Diddy: One of my programmers, he's a big Drum and Bass head. I gave him some acapella's, and he played around with it, and it was incredible. Besides that, the time I spent in London, they didn't have any Hip-Hop songs from the beginning when I was going there. I used to go to Jungle and Drum and Bass clubs. I'm Black, from Africa, a descendant of Africa, and it just reminded me of home.

Who is remixing that?

Diddy: Marc Pfafflin (DJ Fafu)

What was your biggest inspiration behind **Forever**?

Diddy: My biggest inspiration was doing it again. The disbelief that it could be done again. That always drives me. The odds against me always drive me because I'm a believer that it's gonna get to a point where I'm gonna make everybody give up. I'll make everybody give up on hating. 'No, no. Don't hate on him 'cause he's not gonna stop.' It's almost like you'll be this little kid on the football team, and he'll be the smallest guy, but he'll be the hardest worker, the hardest tackler. And it's like when you get in front of him you could be 100lbs bigger than him, but you'll be 'Oh my God, why am I with him? He's gonna bite at my leg. He's gonna grab on to me. He's gonna go all out the whole game. I'd rather be in front of somebody else.' That's the way I want them to look at me when they see me coming. It's like, he's never gonna stop.

CHAPTER 6

LATIN LINGO

You have a lot of support in the Latin community. Will we see a new Latin video?

Diddy: I've done four videos for the first single, "P.E. 2000." I did a video in Spanish; I did a rock video with Chuck D;, and I did a Spanglish video, Spanish and English. I'm not fluent in Spanish, at all. The reason why I did that is that on my first album I had a song called "Senorita" on my album, so I did this two-and-a-half year before Ricky Martin blew up. Everybody that thinks I used my business savvy to exploit the Latin market I did this before. I did the show in my concerts in the Latin heavy populated markets, and the love that I got, the response I got for doing a song and recognising their language, recognising their culture was overwhelming. And a big part of my sales is from the Latin community, so I said when I did my first single I would do like… I would pay respect to the Latin community. You could tell that I don't speak Latin, Spanish. It's more something this is cute, and we gonna get the video, and you got to check it out.

Does it have anything to do with dating Jennifer Lopez?

Diddy: No. She helped me with the song though, but it had nothing to do with her influence. Personally, we're friends. We treat each other like friends.

CHAPTER 7

P. DIDDY LOVES THE KIDS

My son is eight years old. He's into Boomtang Boys, Britney Spears. Is there gonna be anything on **Forever** for him?

Diddy: Yeah. As he's graduating his musical ear, as it's evolving I would have to say, I may be the next step for him. I have a song on there, which I did for the kids, is called "My Best Friend," which is about my relationship with God. I feel like on my albums I show kids all sides of me. I say bad words. I do provocative things at times, and I show you the good, bad and ugly side of me. I've also shown kids the side me that I get on my knees every day and I pray and I thank God for being where I'm at. You have a song on there, "I'll Do This For You," which is myself and Kelly Price, which is real hot and danceable. There's a bunch of stuff. You have Redman on there, Busta Rhymes, all of the cats he will probably be into; Biggie and Lil Kim. Also, we made a clean album for kids that were eight years old. No curse and no -

No explicit lyrics sticker?

Diddy: Oh yeah, on the regular album. I'm an adult. I

make music for adults, but I have fans that are kids, so I've done an album whereas I've covered up all the curses. But also, I took out any indication of violence or explicit sexuality, so it's not just the cuss words that are taken out. It's also the words that would also lead to anything that a kid may not have a chance to understand and digest.

No Way Out, three or four versions were floating around at some point. Does it compromise your artistic integrity that you take something you want to say and then modify it?

Diddy: I'm a Father. I'm a Father first before I get behind the mic and I have a responsibility. Other artists, they may not want to do that, but as a Father, I hurt one of my kids. My son Justin, he had said one of my raps, and he had said one of the bad words by accident. It was just an accident. He didn't know what it meant. It was nothing bad or evil. It was just he said the word shit, and he didn't understand that's what I said on one of the records, and as a parent it made me be like you can't take it for granted. They all gonna repeat what you gonna say, and I just want them to repeat the version of the album that doesn't have the curses on it.

You're an inspiration. You're 29 now. You had many milestones in your 20's. What would you say to kids in their late teens who are kept down?

Diddy: I would tell them they have to fight. Don't accept being kept down. Don't accept being an intern, accept being in the mailroom. You have to fight to be the best intern and best mailroom person, whereas people take notice of what you're doing and how much you love what you're doing. Believe me, your work will speak for itself. You don't have to worry about money; you won't have to worry about advancement. It will come to you. People will be beating down your door.

Are you involved with any youth programs?

Diddy: Yes, I just became a spokesman for America's Promise (Alliance), Colin Powell's organisation, General Colin Powell, and I have Daddy's House for underprivileged children, which is my own charity organisation.

What does America's Promise do?

Diddy: It talks to troubled youths all over the United States. Janet Jackson was the spokesman last year.

What role do you have? Is there a mandate?

Diddy: I have to speak to as many kids as they can find time in my schedule that we coordinate that are troubled.

What will you tell them?

Diddy: I would tell them so much. I would tell them that as a person that's made mistakes, a person that wasn't supposed to make it out of certain things. That a person who could have went in this direction, went in that direction, and that it's time for them to grow up and be leaders and to make a change and not just to give up to the statistics or what they supposed to be. I don't care if you've been locked up three times and got two felonies on your third strike. If you want to, you can turn that all the way around tomorrow and be a lawyer. Regardless, everybody has different cards dealt for them. Everybody has problems. Even kids that are born with money and wealth. That doesn't mean they're gonna turn out to be good people. In my albums and my records, even though I talk about money at times, I also talk about the personal side of things. I'm a Rap artist; I'm proud to say I touch on stuff that people would be afraid to talk about. Whether it's God; whether it's how they died this day or felt this day; when they girlfriend left them or the pain. I'm not afraid to talk about those things, and it's important that kids know that they can make it out of anything. It's how they have to be in control of their own destiny, and it doesn't matter. They have to try to be the best person they can be, and everything else will come naturally, even if you don't get it in the form of money. You'll get it in the form of Heaven, being able to go to sleep at night.

CHAPTER 8

THE REAL DIDDY

Image versus reality.

Diddy: A lot of things what you see is what you get. How I live, how I am. It's a lot of the personal things as far as me as a person, the shades off, or maybe being silly, acting silly, acting stupid. Some of that stuff doesn't come across as much, but on this album, a lot more of me is going to come across. What you see isn't a facade of something fictional. What you see is what I am, whether you like it or not. It's close; it's a piece of what I am. It's not the whole component, but it's a piece of what I am.

What do you want to put out there? What do you want people to know about you?

Diddy: This time I want to put out there that... I want to take my shades off basically, so I took them off and let them see my eyes and let them understand who I am because I don't think I'll be able to sleep knowing that I did some records and I didn't let people... I blocked people from getting inside of me. I want people to get inside me and have their hands in it, whether they like me or not. I at least want to let them know that they got the true me, I mean, all of me.

What is it?

Diddy: As long as it's been, I'm a person that's very diverse, that's caring, that's loving, that's passionate, that's aggressive, that has a good and a bad side. I have faults. I have success'. I'm a real person. I can't cast no stones on nobody. I'm not no better because I made some records and made some money than the next individual. I'm the same human being that's trying to survive and win the game of life at the end of the day like everybody else.

You've been in the game a decade and won most of the time. How do we know you're real? How do we know you're sincere? And, how do we know you're not in it for self?

Diddy: I guess you got to wait and see. I can't prove that to you but through my actions. My actions is that there's a certain amount of reality. I got into the music industry as an intern. There was no such thing as an intern. There was no such thing as young Black people having their own record companies, except for me. Eazy-E had his. Besides that, I don't know of that many.

Rap-A-Lot, Luke.

Diddy: Rap-A-Lot. I'm talking about I was 19 years old.

As far as changing the game of the executives, more on the executive front of opening doors for young executives, from the magazine side of things to the music, to the production side of things. I try to make people believe. That was one of my motivations that the music was for young people and they should at least have some control in it. Besides that, I don't think that you could go that far if your motivation is just money because after you get a certain amount of money, which I've seen a lot of money, it becomes boring to you. If my motivation was money, I could retire right now and never work another day. My kids would never have to work another day as long as I kept the money in good investments and good banks with no Y2K problems or anything like that. My motivation is entertaining people, open up doors and breaking down barriers. You would have to see that, but I wouldn't care what you or anybody else felt or judged about me. God can only judge me. That's it.

What is the drawback of reaching the stature that you've reached?

Diddy: I don't think there's any drawbacks. Even the amount of pressure and the amount of hate, and the amount of jealousy.

The amount of privacy. You can't walk around.

Diddy: You only can't walk around if you don't want to walk around. If you act like a big star, then people will treat you like a big star. I know how to turn that switch on and off. If I want to feel like a big star one day, then I act like a big star. If I want to jump in my car and go to the hood, then it would be good to take one security guard with me. I would advise that. So, I would go to a party or whatever. It's not like I don't go to the clubs, I don't do some of the same things that I used to do, I still stay in touch, but beyond that, I still ask questions. Cousins, friends, little kids, what you like, and to the adults I'm always a question asking person. I'm always in search of knowledge.

Do you listen to any Soul music?

Diddy: Yeah, that's my favourite music to listen to, to be honest. That's how it influences me with Hip-Hop. Marvin Gaye is my favourite artist in the whole wide world.

What about new Soul?

Diddy: Mary J. Blige, Lauryn Hill.

CHAPTER 9

FAITH

You say you pray every day. At what point in your career, and there have been a lot of ups and downs, do you realise it was God who was responsible for all your success and not you, the person.

Diddy: I've always realised that. I've been blessed that my grandmother brought me up in the church, and also, I went to private school, I was an altar boy, and through all of that, I never became a religious person. I never was in love with the whole preacher thing.

You're spiritual.

Diddy: Yeah, I became through that. I gained a relationship with God where I would talk to him almost like a person talk to themselves because I truly believe in him. I was born with that. I never had to find God. I always believed and had 100% faith in him.

What is the misconception people have about you?

Diddy: There's a lot of people that don't know me. I don't, as far as the misconceptions, I don't get into them like that. If somebody doesn't want to know you and doesn't take time to get to know you, they gonna have their misconceptions, if people try to read too deep into things. If there's any misconception sometimes, you could also be responsible. I could be responsible for my own misconception. The Steve Stoute incident, you be misconceived that I have a temper problem, or I'm a thug. I could have added to that misconception. I talk about money on my records. You could just take that I like money or I'm materialistic. I could have added to that, but I would rather talk about something positive, or something that would have kids want to work hard to get this or that. Instead of them talking about how mad I am, or living in the projects, or you could talk about. You could have a misconception about anything if you want to read that deep into something, but, if you want to know and care about somebody, you have to view someone as a human being. This person is not perfect. This person is gonna have some things about him or her that I don't like, and I got to judge that person like how I want him to judge me. Even though I shouldn't be judging, because it's in the Bible that I should cast no stones.

Did you have anything to do with Mase's decision to do what he's doing now? (*On April 20, 1999, Mase retired from the music business to pursue his calling from God.*)

Diddy: No, I had nothing to do with his decision. That was his own decision as a man.

Did you talk to him about it?

Diddy: Yeah, I talked to him about it and I told him, if that's what he feels in his heart, he should follow his heart because after all this money going after all these hit records going, it's gonna be him and the mirror standing there. He has to be able to live with himself. You have to be happy, so I'm 100% supportive of that. I wish we didn't do an album. I wish we didn't just finish an album, but that's the way it goes. We've made a lot of hit records together and a lot of money, and if he ever changes his mind, he's more than welcome to come rock with me.

Was that brought up out of the blue?

Diddy: It was brought out of the blue, I was blown away. It just brought up out of the blue, and you know

CHAPTER 10

RUMOURS

How do you deal with all the rumours? You have the most rumours of anybody of all-time.

Diddy: I laugh at most of the rumours. Some of them get me upset. I handle them as rumours. Deep down inside I know that they're not true. The ones that are true, some rumours have been true, which I don't remember, but, I deal with it day-by-day, rumour by rumour.

You're on top, and people are trying to knock you down.

Diddy: I don't know the rankings of who's on top with all of that, but I know that once you reach a certain status, it's more money, more problems coming into effect. People try to knock you when you are making movements; they try to knock you backwards.

There's been an unfortunate amount of player hating directed your way. On the Sway and Tech compilation, there's a couple of comments about silver jacket wearing and that sort of thing, and there has been a bit of backlash against the more materialistic elements of what you reintroduced to Hip-Hop the past couple of years.

Diddy: Anything about as far as that, I always invite people to have something to say: be a man. Come, say it to my face. Don't hide behind anything. If you want to say something on a record, say my name. That's number one. Number two is I'm gonna be who I'm gonna be. I don't smoke blunts. I don't do certain things. I'm me. I don't wear fatigues in videos. That's not me, that's not my style, and I don't knock anybody that does that. But, I'm not gonna do that because that's the coolest, hippest underground thing that this cat is doing that this week or that cat is doing this week. I'm an entertainer. I'm a wear some stuff that Hip-Hop is gonna hate, which people are gonna hate, and I'm gonna wear some stuff that people are gonna love. I'm gonna do things that they love and hate. I'm gonna always be pushing the limit. I'm gonna always be going into waters that kids, cats with no heart are afraid to do. They want to stay and keep it real and all that. I'm keeping it real with me. I know who I am and I'm a shiny suit wearing, jean, Bentley driving, Hip-Hop club ripping…

Some of the criticism is how "All About The Benjamins" brings it away from the street.

Diddy: In that song we didn't even talk about no money, to be honest. Kids know how we make records. Half the time the chorus has nothing to do with the verses. It was something that -

The general attitude you project is one of wealth, a certain amount of status, and it seems to be that is directed towards being the pinnacle, being the apex, being what you really should strive for. As opposed to more general positive or political -

Diddy: I'm saying you're right. That's what I do.

You never question that?

Diddy: No, that's me. I'm not Chuck D but Chuck D's my man, we could rap on a record together. I'm not KRS-One, I'm not Mobb Deep, I'm not Jay-Z, and I ain't nobody on the Sway and Tech compilation. I'm Puff Daddy; I'm me. If you don't like the things I talk about or choose to talk about, then you shouldn't buy it.

Sway and King Tech released the 32-track compilation **This Or That**, June 15, 1999, on Interscope Records.

Chapter 11

BLACK SINATRA

Your Black Sinatra tag. Initially, that was something you were cool too, but then you embraced?

Diddy: I didn't understand it because I didn't know about Sinatra's life. Chuck D would call me that and one day they had the A&E Biography special and as it was on my phone with lighting up. People that knew me was 'That's you!' 'All that bad stuff and the good stuff he's doing, that's you.' And then I looked, people sent me the video. I was like, 'Oh, my God.' It was like some similarities. It wasn't exactly. It was just either his bad attitude, like the little certain - or a lot of little details, and it was funny because I had met his daughter, Nancy Sinatra. One of the worst moments of my life, I got nominated for five American Music Awards, and I had performed, I had got the only standing ovation of the show. I didn't win one award. I got shut out, and, I guess, Nancy Sinatra felt bad for me, and when she went to accept her award, she said the only daddy cooler than my daddy is Puff Daddy and then she went on to her speech, and I didn't understand where that came from. So, when they had said that to me, it was like all kind of weird and funny. It's cool. He was a survivor more than anything, and he had some rough times, but eventually, he won. He got his life together. He left here with everybody happy with him.

CHAPTER 12

THE NOTORIOUS B.I.G.

What's going on with the new B.I.G. album?

Diddy: The new B.I.G. album, we're just finishing the production on the album. We get my album out the way and Lil Kim's album out of the way. Since B.I.G. is so big and such a big event, we want to make sure it has its place. But we're finishing production every day, working hard on it every day.

What material is left over? It's important to you to do this artist justice. Are these tracks that maybe he hadn't finished, or -

Diddy: No. Only the tracks that he finished that he loved. The only person that rejected tracks was me, and none of these was rejected tracks. Usually, when we do albums, it's a known fact that we usually over-cut so many that there's only 76 minutes that you can have on a CD, so usually there's other cuts that are left over. None of these is tracks that were rejected or, 'Okay, this isn't good enough for the album.' To be honest, B.I.G. never made a lot of stuff like that. If anything, it was rejected he would always come back and fix it, but he never made a wack record.
Do you have to fix up any of the tracks at all?

Diddy: Musically, I have to update it musically. Stuff that was done six months ago sounds different than the stuff that was done today. I have to update it musically.

What do you think about Big's mother coming out saying Charli Baltimore was not his girl and had nothing to do with Big?

Diddy: I don't get into all the personal stuff about it. Big, he was doing his thing like any man sometimes does his thing. He ain't here to speak for himself, so I don't know how he felt about exactly, what he felt about his girls, and stuff like that.

Do you know what's going on now with the investigation? Is there anything new at all? What positive has affect has come out of all this?

Diddy: I don't know about anything new. It's not like the Police call me. I have read the same thing you all have read from the L.A. Times, and besides that, I haven't anything since that, and there's nothing positive that has come out of it for me.

What is with all these conspiracy theories?

Diddy: I'm not sure about which conspiracies.

The whole 2Pac and B.I.G. thing.

Diddy: Those are - That's just bullshit, to be honest. I don't know... I guess people just come up with conspiracy theories. There is no truth in those. I don't even think there's no basis to any of it. That's people talking.

Bad Boy Records released a posthumous The Notorious B.I.G. album **Born Again** on December 7, 1999.

CHAPTER 13

SEX, MONEY & VIOLENCE

What role does sex play in your life?

Diddy: I love sex like any other man, I guess. I'm not addicted to it, but I love it like I love… I don't love it as much as I love music, but it's close.

What role does money play?

Diddy: Money, money kind of funds all of the dreams, all of the things that I'm trying to do. It comes back naturally because I love what I do. I'm in love with what I do. That's the role it plays. I'm not the person sitting there counting every dollar, every dime that comes in. I watch the money. I make sure it doesn't get stolen or leave out on its own, but I'm not the person there 'Oh God, I got a $10 cheque today, I got a $10 000 cheque today.' I'm not that person. I'm not on it like that, to be honest. I talk about money and things like that on my records at a time because I would rather talk about things that are more positive, a little bit more fun, as far as talking about everything that's dark.

You have a court date happening next week.

Diddy: That's not gonna be. I had took care of the situation as far as with Steve Stoute. We had made up. He's since gone and dropped the charges, so they need time to make sure, investigation wise, that everything is on the up and up because sometimes when somebody presses charges and then drops them people think that there may be some foul play or something like that. They are going through the motions of doing their investigation realising that we were friends for seven-and-a-half years, realising that nothing was premeditated. Knowing that his jaw wasn't broken, his arm wasn't broken, he wasn't beaten with a bottle.

Wasn't it premeditated? Did you lose your temper?

Diddy: Yeah, I did lose my temper. I got into an altercation. I got into a fight. I didn't commit second-degree assault to be going to jail, and I'm not going to jail, and everything should be dropped in the next couple of weeks. I'm not going to court next week because they don't feel it's necessary and they're working everything out.

CHAPTER 14

HILLARY CLINTON

Is running for political office something you think?

Diddy: I'm running for the ruler of the world right now. I'm staying away from all that. I'm gonna be politically active. It's very important who is gonna be responsible for the world my kids live in. I have to be politically conscious. I may endorse a candidate here or there in the future.

Hillary Clinton?

Diddy: Yeah, I like Hillary Clinton. She'll do a good job though.

Are you a Republican or a Democrat?

Diddy: I'm a Democrat.

CHAPTER 15

THE BIG SECRET: HOW TO BE A SUCCESSFUL PARTY PROMOTER

Back in the day you were a party promoter and earned your reputation in New York City. Can you give up some game on promoting parties?

Diddy: Yeah. I will say the biggest thing about promoting a party, the big secret I can say is don't try to make money for the first three parties. Try to invite people, the right people, the right party people who have the right karma and energy. The party is all about the energy, all about the karma and the vibe. The reason why people have written about a lot of my parties so much is because I'm a true director of that. I concentrate before you get there that you know you have to come, you have to be in good spirits, you have to have no hang ups, you have to come and have a good time. If you know that before you walk in the door? Imagine five hundred people with all that on their mind and a couple of drinks, and the right music, and the right lighting, and the right male/female -

Always more women.

Diddy: Always more women.

How do you maintain once you've done the three

parties, they're successful, and you've been around a few years?

Diddy: You have to keep on dreaming, keep on giving them new innovative ideas. Lighting is key, the music, the sound system, the way it sounds. All of that stuff that bothers you at a party when you go to a party and the light's too dark, you can't see that girl, you squint your eyes. All of that stuff when the music is cracking, or the music is too loud you can't even hear yourself talk, and every last thing. You have to write down what kind of party would I love to be in and that has to be the party that you promote, and you have to stay consistent with it. I'm giving up a lot.

CHAPTER 16

O CANADA

Welcome to Canada.

Diddy: Showing love to the whole Canadian community it's important to me, from when my label first started to me as an artist paying attention to the market out here, and it's only an hour away, so I'm gonna spend more time out here.

Are you familiar with any Canadian urban acts?

Diddy: I don't know about the whole music scene or what's coming out here, but I know Deborah Cox, and one of my video directors, Little x, are out here, and probably some other people that I know that I probably don't know are from out here. I'm not really into different scenes. I don't think it's where you from, it's where you at. I don't think that that matters that much. I think the scene as far as the party goers and the people, that scene is getting stronger and stronger as far as Hip-Hop is concerned. It's growing every day.

If you had a demo from Canada would you ignore it?

Diddy: Nah, Nah, not at all. If I had a demo from Japan, I would listen to it. To me, you never know what you gonna hear until you listen to it.

Caribana.

Diddy: We gonna rip that shit to pieces. Whatever show we do, wherever we go, we gonna rip it to pieces. That's one thing we are cocky about, one thing we are confident about, is that we feel we rock the hardest. I'm gonna go the hardest. My crew is gonna go the hardest. We love making people feel good and we gonna do some special things for it. I hope everybody comes and behave and have a good time. All colours, races, religion, everybody is welcome.

Is there anything else?

Diddy: I appreciate the support and love Canada has given me, and that's really on the real. I have to say one of the loudest shows I did was when I was in Canada. The people are great, the vibe is great, the whole scene is growing over there. You can tell like Canada for a minute, like, still, the music scene, the people's understanding of it, the sports scene, the party scene, the social scene, intellectual scene, the style, fashion. Everything is all the way up to par. Beyond that, people love the music and people live the culture and the lifestyle the Canadian way, and I respect that, and I can't wait to get out there and see everybody.

CHAPTER 17

FUTURE

MP3

Diddy: MP3 is interesting. It's gonna be interesting to see how it goes down. It's a lot of money. A lot of corporate gangsters. It's like, somebody saying they're gonna be giving away free liquor during Prohibition. We gonna see how the corporate gangsters are gonna handle it. It's exciting for me for the chance to possibly have a Black based, Black owned distribution system, which is a monopoly on it right now as far as distribution, and it opens up the doors for that in the future. It's a beautiful thing as far as the artists getting their music out there. I'm not against it. As a matter of fact, we are talking to them in discussions about some involvement with it. But overall it will be interesting to see how it goes down.

What are you going to be doing ten years from now?

Diddy: I hope that I can still be the hottest young producer in the game.

How do you want to be remembered?

Diddy: I want to be remembered as somebody that always gave it they all. He went all out, and he opened up a lot of doors.

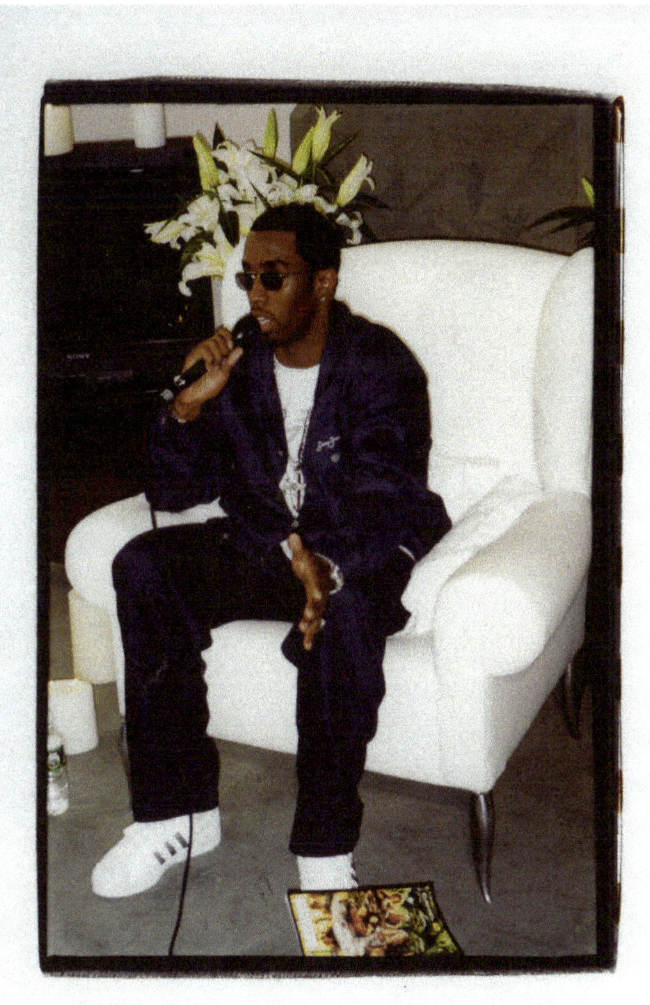

Diddy address' the international media in NYC, June 23, 1999

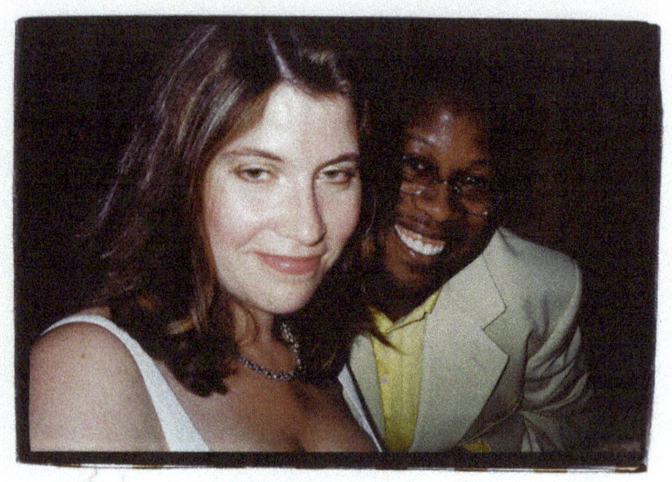

*Former BMG Music Canada President, Lisa Zbitnew and Andre Harrell at the **Forever** international media event, June 23, 1999.*

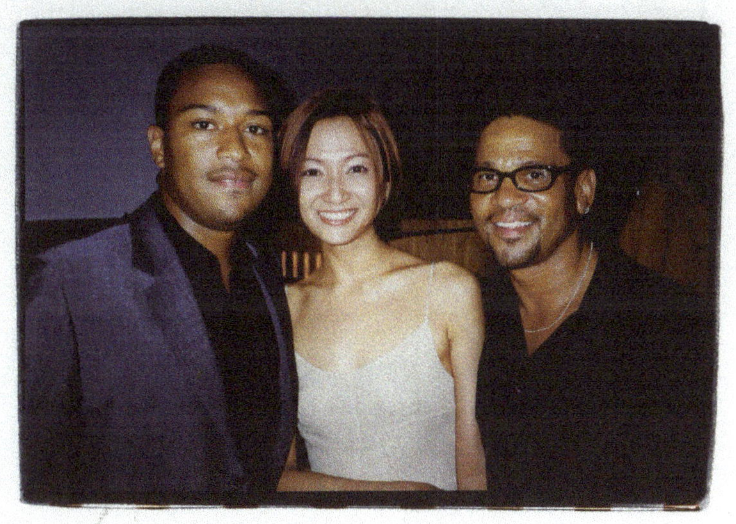

*Benny Medina (glasses) at the **Forever** international media event, June 23, 1999.*

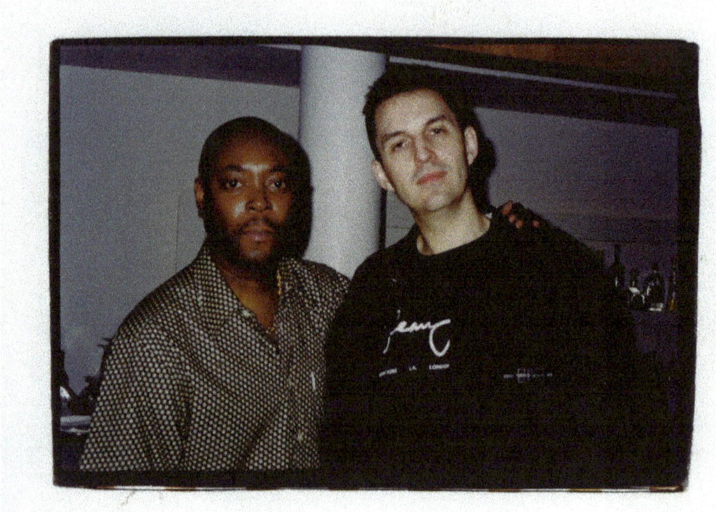

*London, UK radio host and DJ, Jigs, and Tim Westwood, the most influential figure in European Hip-Hop, at the **Forever** international media event, June 23, 1999.*

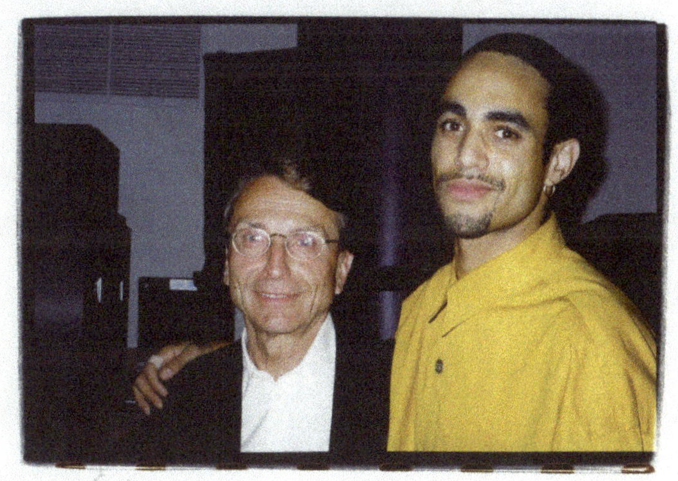

The late Rudi Gassner, former President and CEO of BMG International, and Sol Guy in attendance at the **Forever** *international media event, June 23, 1999.*

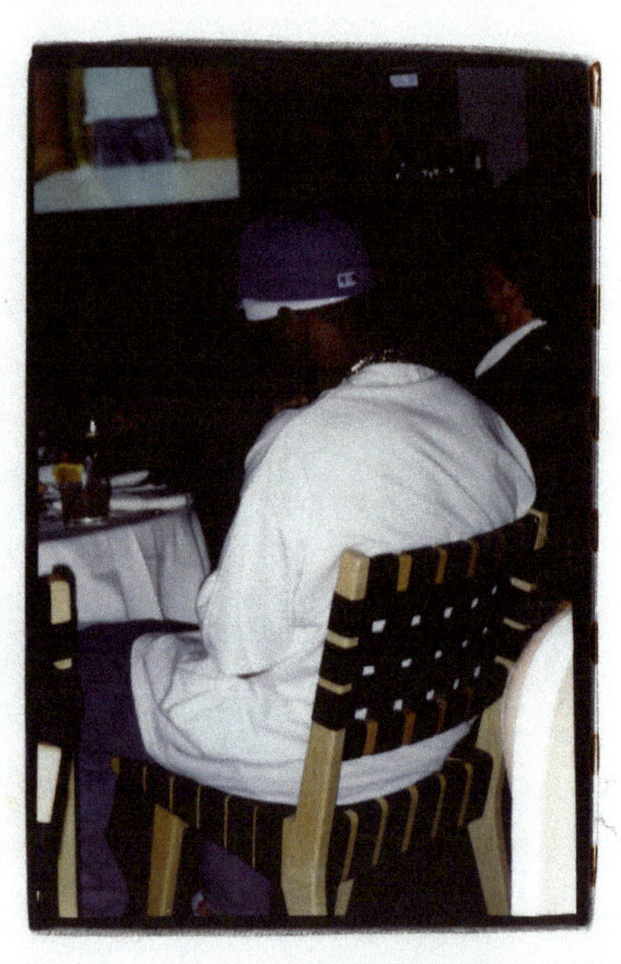

*Diddy sitting down for dinner inside Pop at the **Forever** international media dinner, June 23, 1999.*

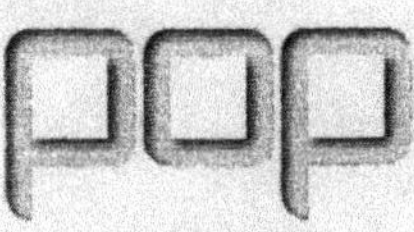

appetizers

choice of
- ginger-marinated shrimp with chinese ratatouille
- wild mushroom soup
- peppered tuna salad with lime vinagrette

entrees

choice of
- sirloin of beef with braised shortrib of beef potato cake
- filet of pop smoked salmon with hijiki-cucumber salad
- broiled lobster with cognac butter

dessert

choice of
- coconut creme caramel with tropical fruit
- bittersweet chocolate cake with pistachio ice cream
- champagne granita with roasted strawberry sorbet

petit fours, coffee & tea

Steak, salmon or lobster?

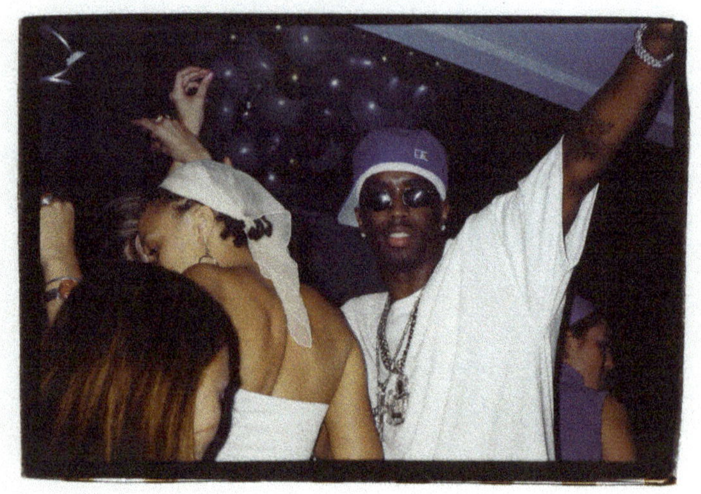

Diddy enjoying the party in NYC, June 23, 1999

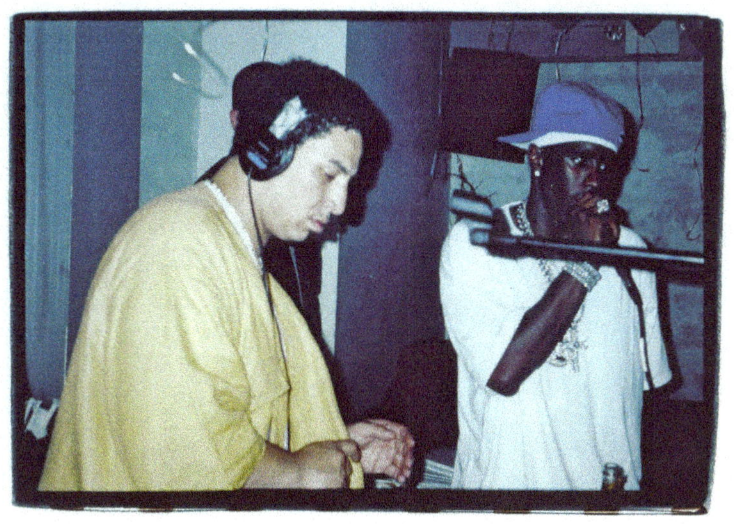

DiddY addressing the party with Kid Capri on the wheels

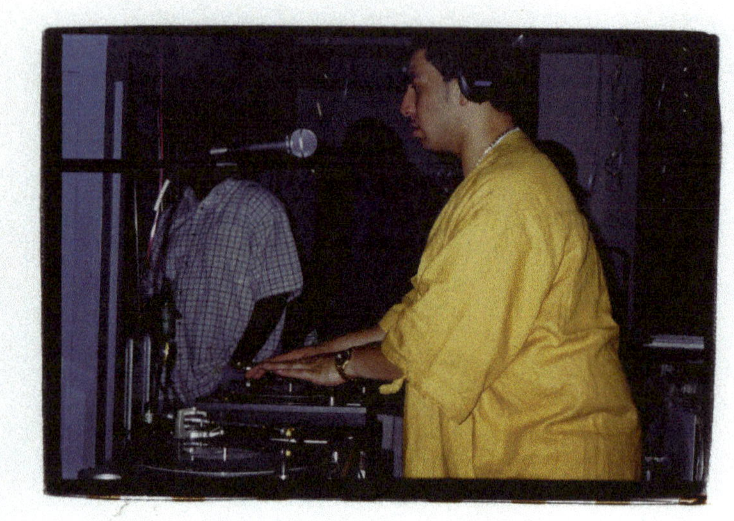

*Kid Capri in the mix at the international media party for **Forever**, June 23, 1999.*

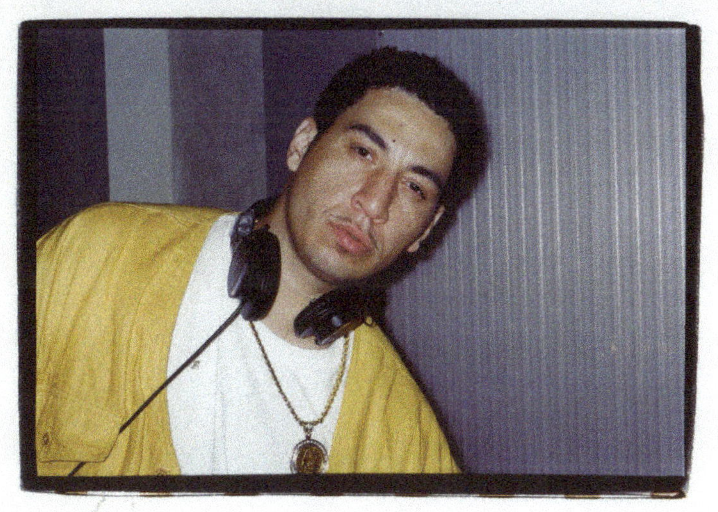

Kid Capri!

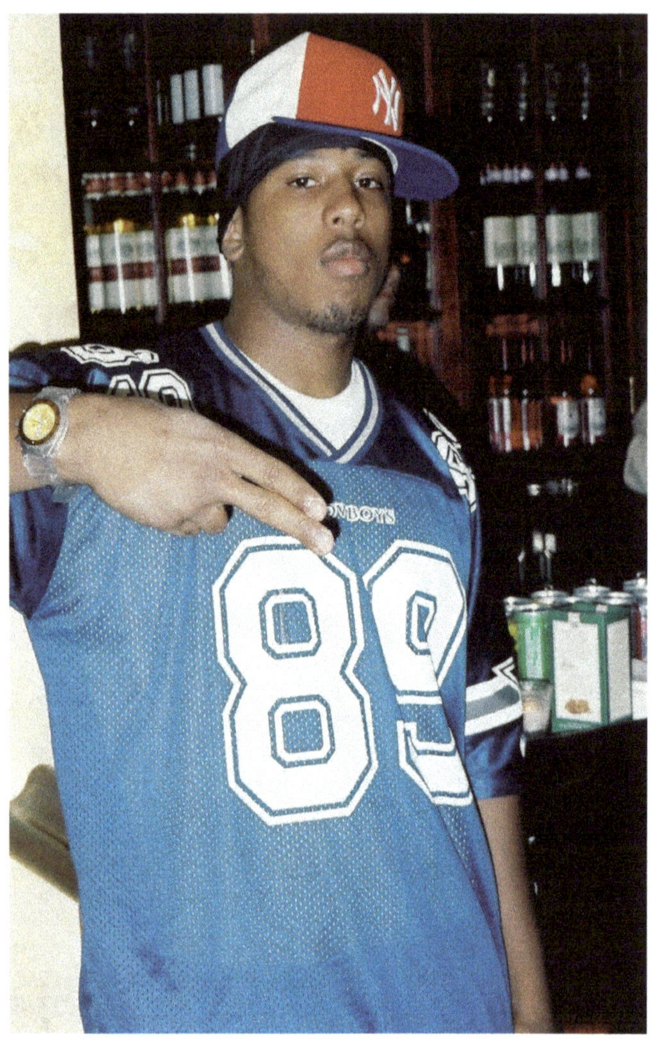

Shyne inside Club Lucky, Toronto, Canada, after the invite-only Puff Daddy **Forever** press conference, July 30, 1999.

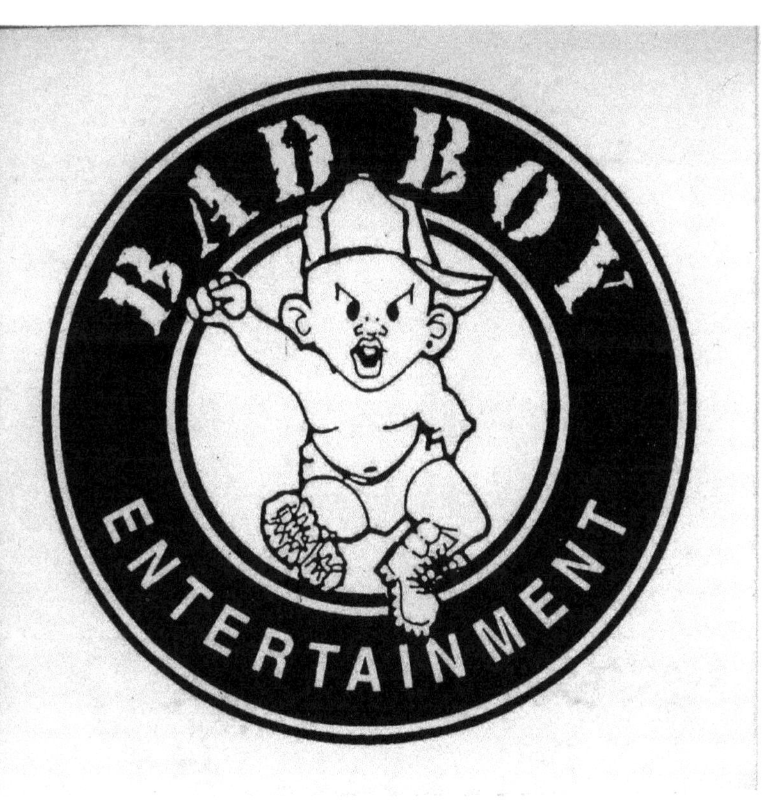

Original 1994 Bad Boy Entertainment sticker

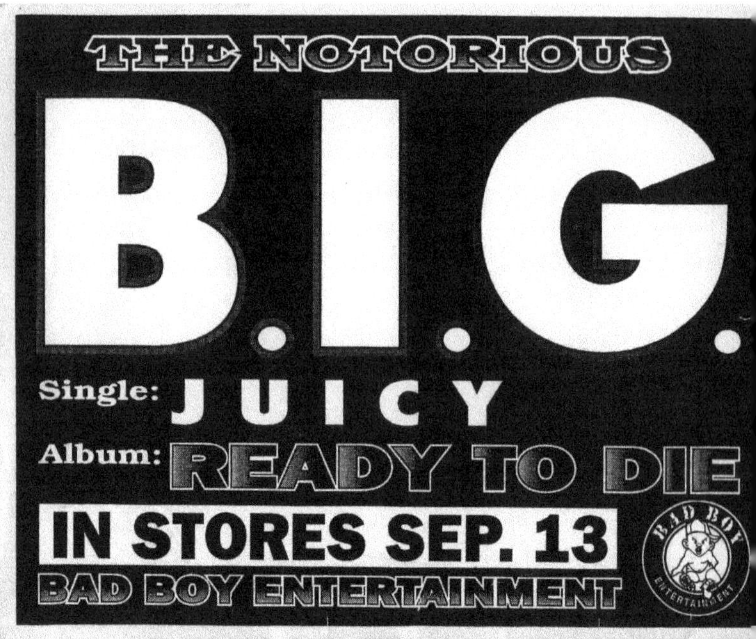

*Original summer 1994 The Notorious B.I.G. Juicy/ **Ready To Die** promotional sticker.*

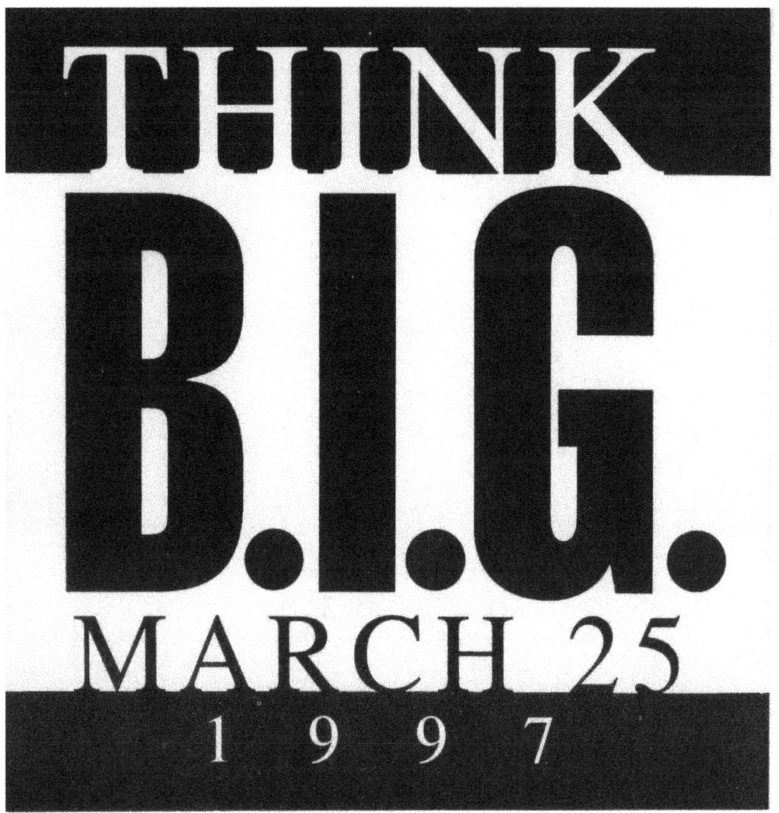

Original The Notorious B.I.G. **Life After Death**
promotional sticker a side

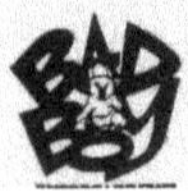

Original The Notorious B.I.G. *Life After Death*
promotional sticker b side

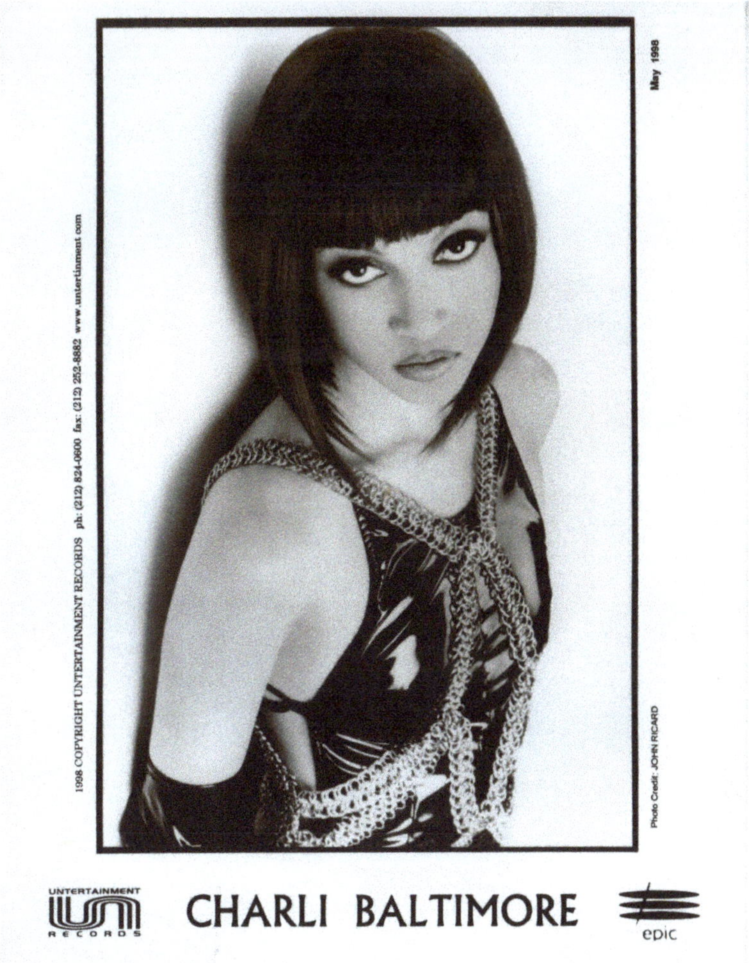

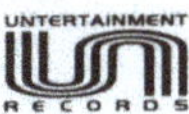
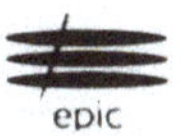

Original 1998 Charli Baltimore promotional pic. Photo by John Ricard.

DISCOGRAPHY

Albums

No Way Out – July 1, 1997 (Bad Boy/Arista)
Forever – August 24, 1999 (Bad Boy/Arista)
The Saga Continues... - June 19, 2001 (Bad Boy/Arista)
Press Play – October 17, 2006 (Bad Boy/Atlantic)
No Way Out 2 coming soon (Bad Boy/Epic)

Collaboration

Last Train To Paris with Dawn Richards – December 14, 2010 (Interscope)
11 11 with Guy Gerber – August 20, 2014 (Rumors)

Remix

We Invented The Remix – May 14, 2002 (Bad Boy/Arista)

Singles

"Can't Nobody Hold Me Down" featuring Mase

"I'll Be Missing You" with Faith Evans featuring 112

"Can't Nobody Hold Me Down" featuring Mase

"I'll Be Missing You" with Faith Evans featuring 112

"It's All About The Benjamins" (Remix) featuring The Notorious B.I.G., Lil' Kim and The Lox

"Been Around The World" featuring The Notorious B.I.G. and Mase

"Victory" featuring The Notorious B.I.G. and Busta Rhymes

"Come With Me" featuring Jimmy Page
"P.E. 2000" featuring Hurricane G

"Satisfy You" featuring R. Kelly

"Do You Like It…Do You Want It" featuring Jay-Z

"Best Friend" featuring Mario Winans

"Bad Boy For Life" featuring Black Rob and Mark Curry

"Diddy" featuring The Neptunes

"I Need A Girl (Part One)" featuring Usher and Loon

"I Need A Girl (Part Two)" featuring Ginuwine, Loon, and Mario Winans

"Let's Get It" featuring Kelis

"Show Me Your Soul" with Lenny Kravitz, Loon, and Pharrell

"Come To Me" featuring Nicole Scherzinger

"Tell Me" featuring Christina Aguilera

"Last Night" featuring Keyshia Cole

"Through The Pain (She Told Me)" featuring Mario Winans

"Angels" with Dirty Money featuring The Notorious B.I.G.

"Love Come Down" with Dirty Money

"Hello Good Morning" with Dirty Money featuring T.I.

"Loving You No More" with Dirty Money featuring Drake

"Coming Home" with Dirty Money featuring Skylar Grey

"Your Love" with Dirty Money featuring Trey Songz

"Ass On The Floor" with Dirty Money featuring Swizz Beatz

"Big Homie" featuring Rick Ross and French Montana

"I Want The Love" featuring Meek Mill

"Finna Get Loose" featuring Pharrell

"Workin'" featuring Travis Scott and Big Sean

ABOUT THE AUTHOR

Father. Son. Brother.

HARRIS ROSEN was born and lives in Toronto, Canada. He is the force and Author of the Behind The Music Tales series. His book N.W.A: The Aftermath was #1 on Amazon in the United States, Canada, France, Australia, and Japan!

For twenty years, he self-published the national lifestyle magazine Peace! He has interviewed hundreds of composers, artists, actors, and athletes, including the Notorious B.I.G., Dr Dre, Daft Punk, Eminem, Derek Jeter, Georges St. Pierre, Nirvana, Metallica, Chris Rock, Buju Banton, Beastie Boys, Kiss, Destiny's Child and Aaliyah to list a few.

He has gone to six continents and was in the midst of a whirlwind of multiple musical, cultural revolutions that occurred throughout the 90's and 2000s while compiling a genuine and honest archive of audio, images and video.

behindthemusictales.com

facebook.com/behindthemusictales

instagram.com/behindthemusictales

twitter.com/mrheller1

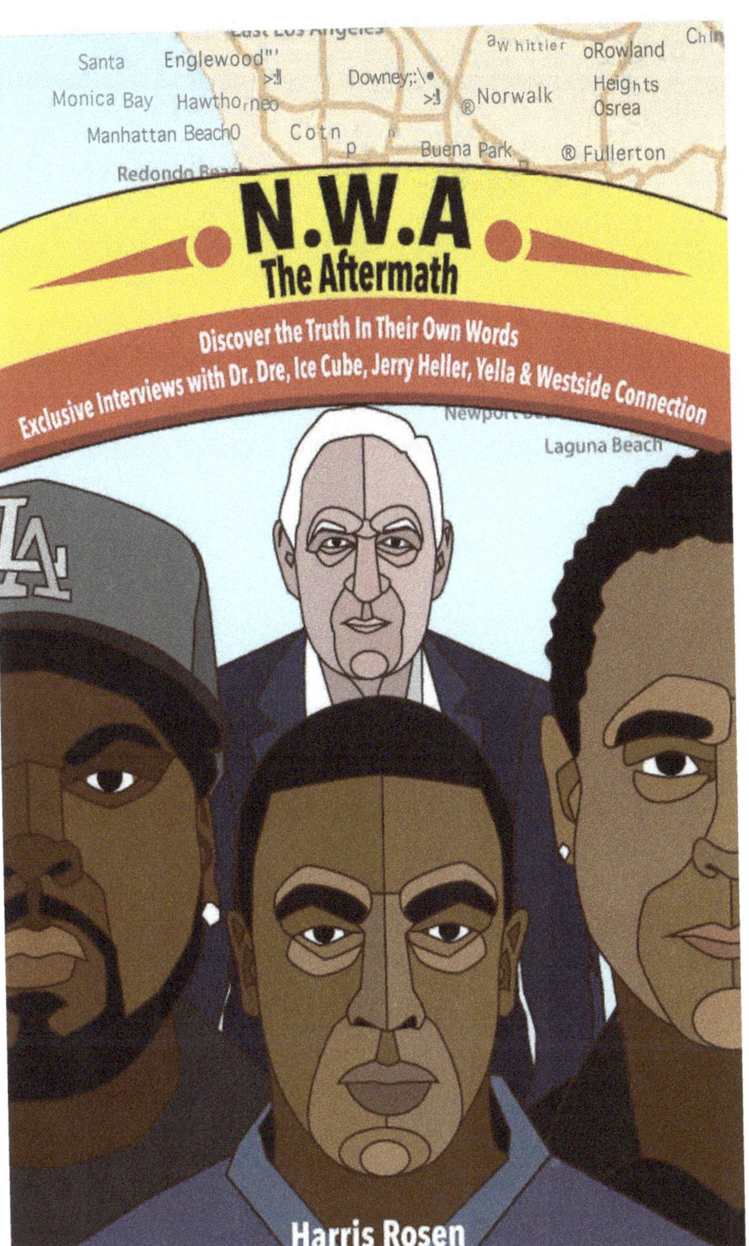

Santa Englewood
Monica Bay Hawthorneo
Manhattan Beach0
Redondo Beach
East Los Angeles
Downey
Norwalk
Buena Park
Whittier oRowland
Heights
Osrea
Fullerton
N.W.A
The Aftermath
Discover the Truth In Their Own Words
Exclusive Interviews with Dr. Dre, Ice Cube, Jerry Heller, Yella & Westside Connection
Newport
Laguna Beach
LA
Harris Rosen

[N.W.A Fans Only!] Astonishing facts revealed for the first time!

DR. DRE: *Tupac never knew me.*
ICE CUBE: *I just do shit for Ice Cube fans, not for Hip-Hop fans.*
YELLA: *Me and Dre produced all Eazy, N.W.A. All of that. Me and him did that together.*
JERRY HELLER: *There are people that think that I am the white Devil.*

N.W.A: The Aftermath is your one-way ticket deep inside the world's most dangerous group. It will blow your mind!

What you will read here has been sensationalised by others in a manner of journalistic psycho-speak. **N.W.A: The Aftermath** is as close to the truth as one can get. It delivers raw thoughts by real people and is manifested directly in the voice and words of the artists who made it happen.

Each chapter will unravel tall tales and give you new insight. Don't miss out on the opportunity to learn what happened.

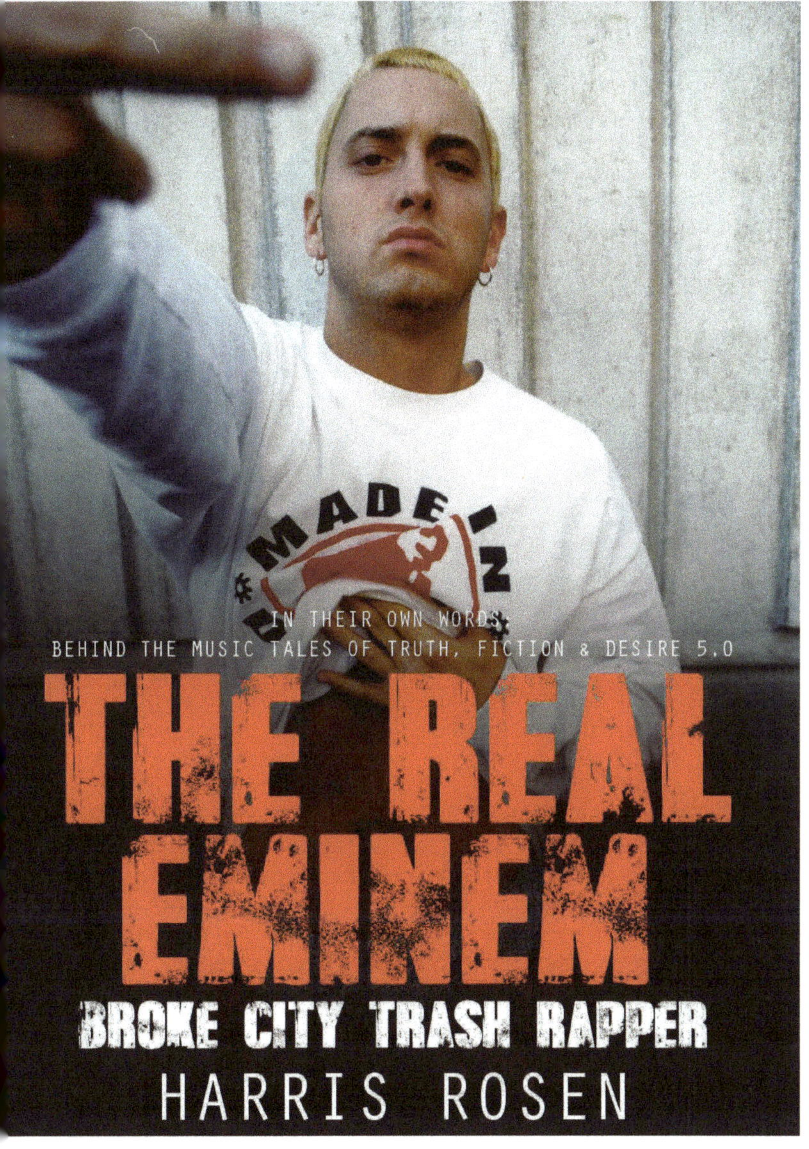
IN THEIR OWN WORDS:
BEHIND THE MUSIC TALES OF TRUTH, FICTION & DESIRE 5.0
THE REAL EMINEM
BROKE CITY TRASH RAPPER
HARRIS ROSEN

Exclusive audio, rare unreleased songs, and interviews with Eminem & D12.

The Real Eminem: Broke City Trash Rapper is your one-way ticket deep inside the mind of the real Eminem. It will blow your mind!

This book contains two exclusive in-person April 1999 interviews with Eminem and one exclusive in-person 2001 interview with D12.

These exclusive, original interviews deliver a raw twenty-six years old Eminem, the real Eminem as an angry young man eager to prove himself to the world and give them the middle-finger at the same time. These interviews deliver an Eminem solely concerned with representing himself, his family, and those he came up with in his moment of need. These accounts produce an Eminem who proudly declared he lived for the day.

Eminem didn't invent ill rhyming or the unfortunate lower class intellect nevertheless, he had lived it, seen it, done it, and was now speaking on it for the world to hear. He was not a bad guy. Everything he wrote, rapped or spoke had been in the mix, in one form or another, before.

The second part of the book features an exclusive 2001 interview with D12. It provides a first-hand look into the "Just Don't Give A Fuck" mindset of the crew and choice background information on Eminem in the midst of becoming an international phenomenon.

THE REAL DESTINY'S CHILD

The Writing's On The Wall

Behind The Music Tales 6.0

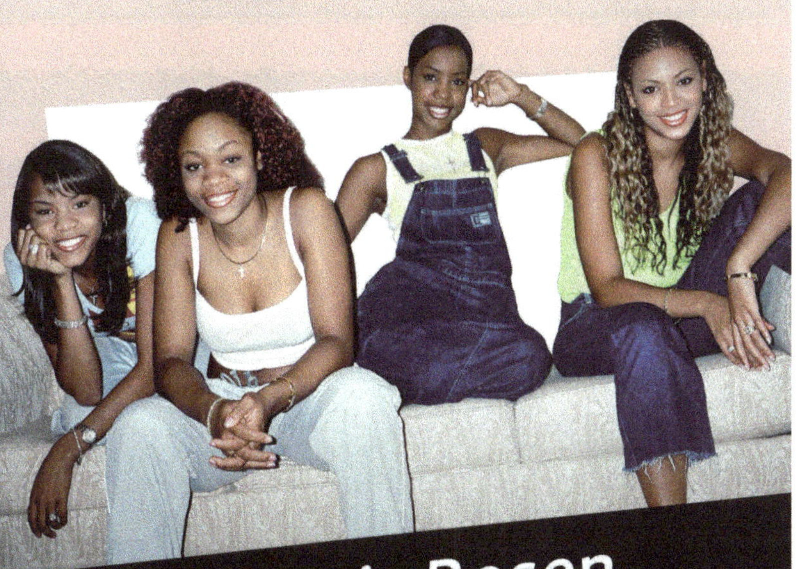

Harris Rosen

An intimate portrait of Destiny's Child and the girl who would be Queen.

A revealing eye on the state of the union of The Real Destiny's Child in the months leading up to their bitter separation. Never before heard revelations leading up to the inconceivable truth.

The Real Destiny's Child at the most pivotal time in their career. This book is straight talk direct from Destiny's Child in their own words. A rare opportunity to go deep Behind The Music Tales and inside their minds documenting **The Writing's On The Wall** album, love, hope, dreams and more. In these pages you'll discover:

EXCLUSIVE spring 1999 casual photo shoot with The Real Destiny's Child

EXCLUSIVE prints from the Bootylicious Remix video

EXCLUSIVE song-by-song breakdown of THE WRITING'S ON THE WALL

EXCLUSIVE interview audio excerpts

Rare pre-teen video auditions, rehearsals, and unreleased songs

Many people know Destiny's Child as one of the most successful groups of all time. Then at the height of their popularity, they broke up. Here they are revealing their struggles for fame and love mere months before the descent and madness.

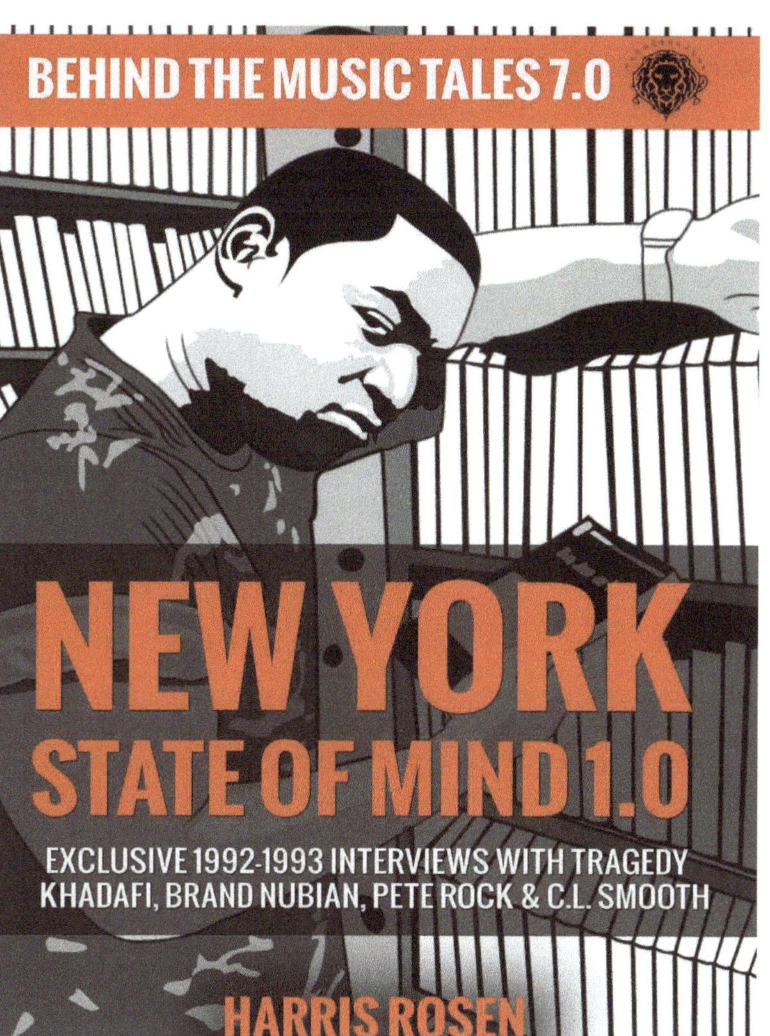

BEHIND THE MUSIC TALES 7.0
NEW YORK
STATE OF MIND 1.0
EXCLUSIVE 1992-1993 INTERVIEWS WITH TRAGEDY
KHADAFI, BRAND NUBIAN, PETE ROCK & C.L. SMOOTH
HARRIS ROSEN

A fascinating genuine narrative formed in the crucible of Golden Age Hip-Hop mindfulness.

New York State of Mind 1.0, the 7th book in the series, provides you with a real flavour of the personalities, in all their raw forms, who breathed life into the streets of the city, taking the music to new heights and in radically new directions.

Tragedy Khadafi is as real as it gets. Through impressive MC skills and a formidable street reputation, he lived the life of an original hoodlum, surviving gunshot wounds, stabbings and broken bones. The compelling lyrical message of Brand Nubian reflects on the group's identity as Five-Percenters and the philosophy of the Nation of Gods and Earth, while Pete Rock & C.L. Smooth arrived on the scene in the midst of a Hip-Hop impasse of sorts.

New York State of Mind 1.0 is a candid look deep inside the psyche of each and an examination of what makes them tick. Take a ride alongside them and learn how they made their mark in a generation.

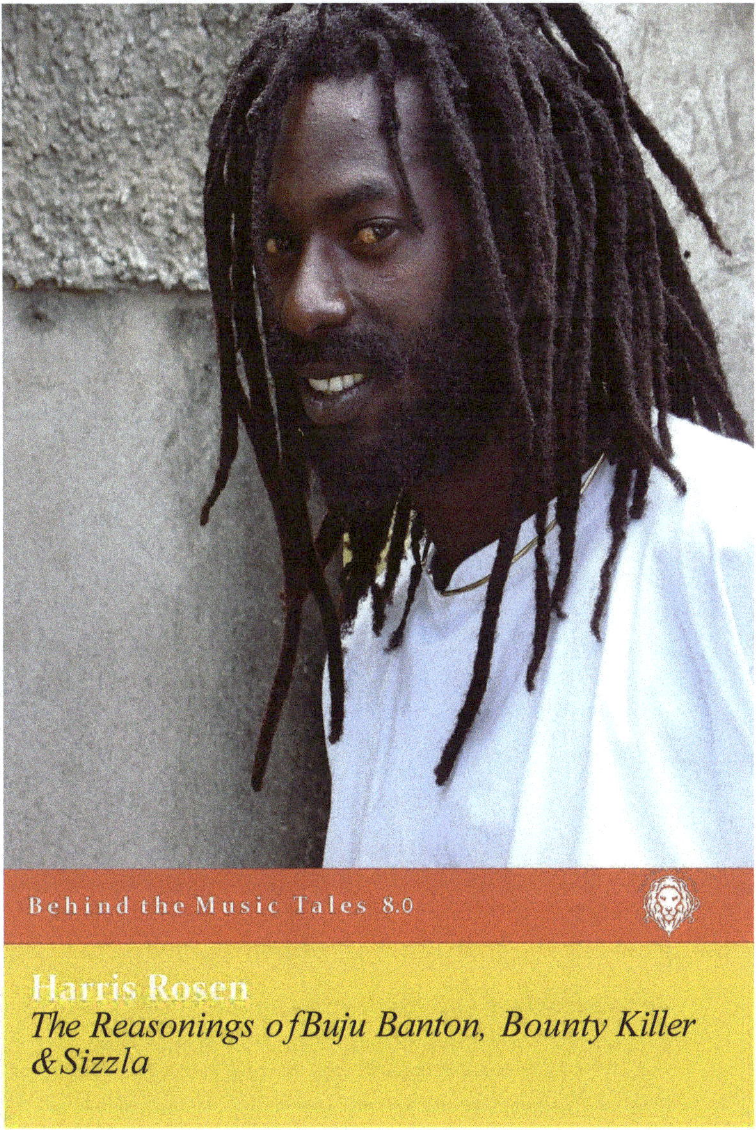

Behind the Music Tales 8.0

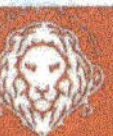

Harris Rosen

The Reasonings of Buju Banton, Bounty Killer & Sizzla

An engaging literal account of how three prodigious talents ply and impact a nation of millions with their reactionary music.

Now, in **The Reasonings of Buju Banton, Bounty Killer & Sizzla**, the 8th book in the series, you can get inside the minds of some of the most significant artists who have made their mark on Reggae music for generations to come.

Buju Banton is one of these men. A certified natural talent, his career was hallmarked by his socio-political and overtly sexual lyrics. Then he turned his back and became a devout Rastafarian. Today, he's imprisoned.

Bounty Killer is acknowledged far and wide as The Warlord. His commanding delivery, attitude and streetwise outlaw music made him one of the biggest stars of his generation. He has likewise spoken candidly about the state of Reggae music and what was keeping it back from crossing over to the masses. Then he faced his most formidable opponent, ever.

Sizzla has released over 60 albums and is respected worldwide for his music. He has actively engaged a youthful following with his spiritual Rastafarian teachings and lifestyle, educating them on corruption, oppression and how to uplift themselves.

The Reasonings of Buju Banton, Bounty Killer & Sizzla, is a rare treat. It captures the thoughts and hopes of artists who have made it their lives to bring one of the most popular forms of music to a much wider audience.

Behind the Music Tales 9.0

48 Exclusive Photos

MAGNOLIA

Home of tha Soldiers

Exclusive interviews with the Hot Boys and Cash Money Millionaires

HARRIS ROSEN

A riveting historical account of how two hustlers invested everything in one ten years old and changed the music business, forever!

Magnolia: Home of tha Soldiers, the 9th book in the series, is a look at how Cash Money Records produced some of the iconic stars of the last two decades and continued to cash in on the day. Get raw and real Lil Wayne, B.G., Juvenile, and Turk revelations of their teen years. Learn how Mannie Fresh created all Cash Money Records music. Put some "respek" on Birman's name. Unmask the mystery of CEO "Slim" and discover the keys to success in an ultra rare enlightening interview.

Magnolia: Home of tha Soldiers is a very authentic account of being a young Black man hustling to put food on the table while fighting for his place in the music scene. It gets the answers you want, from a group of young artists who have had to fight and struggle every day to get what they wanted and to be where they are.

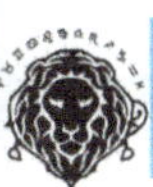

THE REAL 213

by Harris Rosen

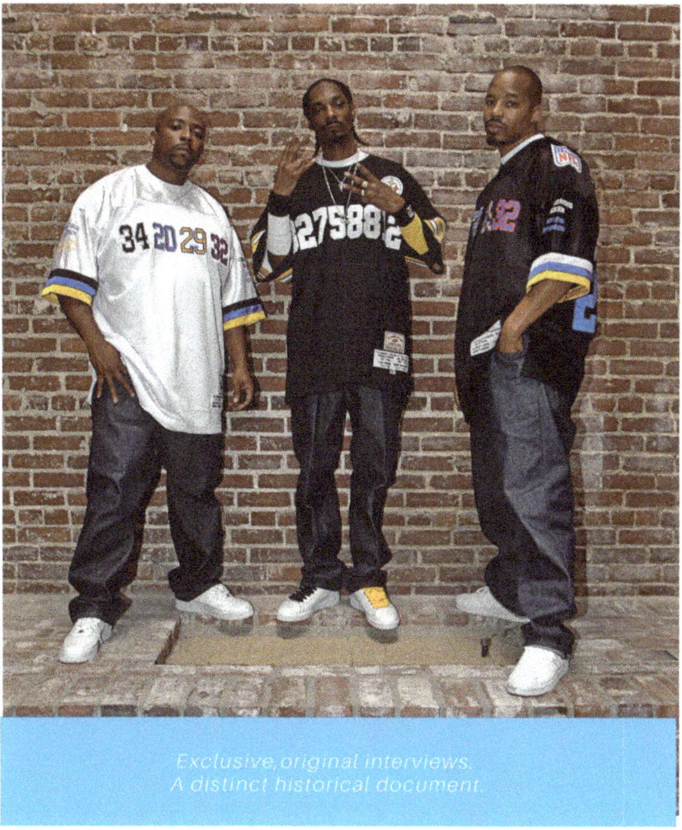

Exclusive interviews and photos with Snoop Dogg, Nate Dogg, Warren G, and Bishop Don Magic Juan. An All-Star cast on an unflinching mission to advance the gospel of their enduring legacy, and the case of G-funk. It ain't no joke!

The Real 213, the 10th book in the series, presents the friendship of Snoop, Nate Dogg and Warren G, one of the most enduring legacies in Hip-Hop history. Innovative. Fearless. Controversial. Outrageous. These interviews with 213 at the intersection of their careers, exposes irony, rhythms, and prejudices of the music business.

Pointed against the political, economic and cultural backdrop of G-funk, **The Real 213** depicts what was to become a pivotal transitional moment in West Coast Rap history. More than six years after the death of Nate Dogg, the distinct style and profound influence of G-funk is indisputable. The pulse has changed. The place stays the same. Chuuch!

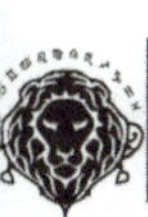

The Real
MC EIHT: GEAH!

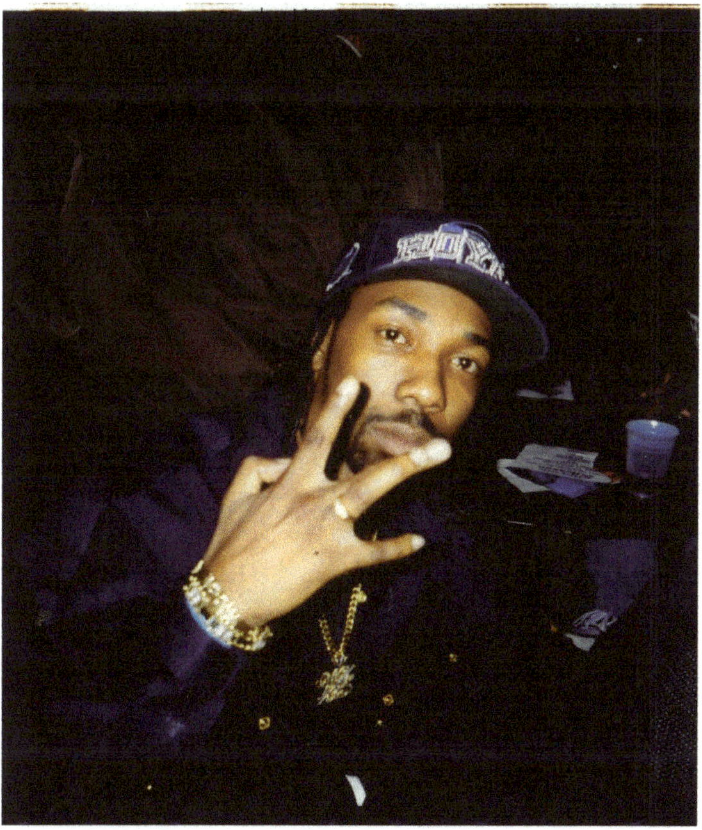

Exclusive, original interviews.
A distinct historical document.

MC Eiht = Reality Rap. Enter the underbelly of Compton and discover the keys to success and longevity in the music game.

The Real MC Eiht: Geah!, the 11th book in the series, is more than an interview with a rapper. It's the key to building a career of longevity in the music game. By telling his story, MC Eiht reveals much about the path to success, and he does so in compelling fashion.

Stating core philosophies - of how to be a man, how to be professional, and how to give fans what they want to hear - the valuable insight, strong convictions and raw determination of MC Eiht address issues that are important to all us of, not just fans of Gangster Rap.

The Real MC Eiht: Geah! captures one of Rap's most enduring and relevant artists. It is the tale of a certified foundation artist straight outta Compton, who has made his mark on Reality Rap and music for the generation to come and continues to contribute to the Art Form to this day.

DOWNLOAD
NEW YORK STATE OF MIND 1.0
FREE!

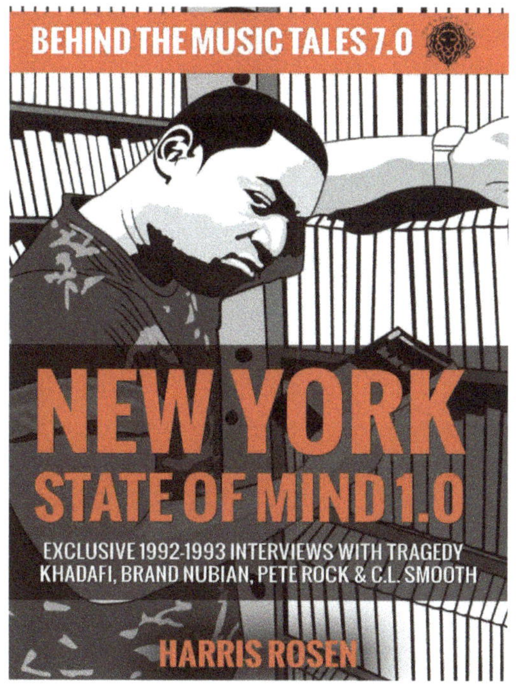

There are hundreds of interviews and dozens of Behind The Music Tales series books to follow. That's why I am giving you a copy of **New York State of Mind 1.0** for FREE!

JOIN THE READERS GROUP AND get exclusive 1992 and 1993 interviews with Tragedy Khadafi, Brand Nubian, and Pete Rock & C.L. Smooth FREE!

I am only looking for your email. You will receive emails with updates on new releases, exclusive images, original audio, and free advance copies of series books. You can opt out at any time.

<http://eepurl.com/ckHZdb>

www.ingramcontent.com/pod-product-compliance
Lightning Source LLC
LaVergne TN
LVHW052243150726
843469LV00054B/2192

* 9 7 8 1 9 8 8 9 5 6 0 0 8 *